# Colossians

## Jesus at the Center of It All

A Read with Me Bible Study from Mabbat Press
by
E. Anne Weil

COLOSSIANS: JESUS AT THE CENTER OF IT ALL
Copyright © 2020 E. Anne Weil

Published by Mabbat Press

Print Edition ISBN-13: 978-1-7350103-1-1

All rights reserved. No part of this publication may be reproduced, stored in a retrieval system, or transmitted in any form or by any means – electronic, mechanical, digital, photocopy, recording, or any other – except for brief quotations in printed reviews, without the prior permission of the publisher.

Scripture quotations are taken from the Holy Bible, New Living Translation, copyright © 1996, 2004, 2015 by Tyndale House Foundation. Used by permission of Tyndale House Publishers, Inc., Carol Stream, Illinois 60188. All rights reserved.

Unless otherwise credited, all photos and artwork by E. Anne Weil.

For more information or to book a speaking event, please write:
Mabbat Press, 1017 Ivy Creek Trail, Hoover, Alabama 35226
or visit our website at mabbat.com.

# Colossians ~

a letter of Paul explaining that Jesus is the center of everything

## The Big Idea:

Jesus is central to and supreme over all creation. He is the visible image of God and the Creator. We have the fullness of Christ when we submit to him.

---

For God in all his fullness was pleased to live in Christ, and through him God reconciled everything to himself. He made peace with everything in heaven and on earth by means of Christ's blood on the cross. Colossians 1:19-20

---

You have died with Christ, and he has set you free from the spiritual powers of this world. So why do you keep on following the rules of the world? Colossians 2:20

---

Put on your new nature, and be renewed as you learn to know your Creator and become like him. In this new life, it doesn't matter if you are a Jew or a Gentile, circumcised or uncircumcised, barbaric, uncivilized, slave, or free. Christ is all that matters, and he lives in all of us. Colossians 3:10-11

---

Pray for us, too, that God will give us many opportunities to speak about his mysterious plan concerning Christ. That is why I am here in chains. Pray that I will proclaim this message as clearly as I should. Colossians 4:3-4

# Welcome to the *Read with Me* series from Mabbat Press.

I hope in these pages you'll find a fresh way to study and interpret God's word in your life. It's probably safe to say that in my lifetime, especially growing up in church, that I've worked through hundreds of Bible study books. I learn something new every time I study with the intent to seek God's face through what I read, but most of those studies didn't help me connect one of the biggest parts of my character (and God's) to my study: creativity.

I love to write - poetry, fiction, essays, anything with words. I love to create art - drawing, painting, crafting, anything involving art supplies (except for knitting - somehow two needles is incomprehensible to my brain..). I loved craft projects when I was a kid in Vacation Bible School or special days in Sunday School, but as an adult craft supplies and Bible study were never connected. Creative writing and Bible study were definitely never connected.

Several years ago, I decided to start a small group at my church for people like me who wanted to explore creativity as a means of worship and learning more about God's character through his written word. It's not a new idea: as long as there has been scripture to study, it has been the inspiration for works of art and music. Recently there's been a Bible journaling trend to create art in the pages of Bibles, and it's all wonderful.

God is first recorded in our history of him as The Creator, spinning the universe from emptiness into the fullness of creation with just words. Then he created us in his image, which means we all have creative abilities. We are created to create. We are created to glorify God with new ideas, to worship him through our practice of the artistry he gifted to us, to display his creative character through our own exploration of creativity.

This series of studies is geared towards writing and visual art prompts because those are my gifts. Whether you have writing or drawing talent or not, you can still practice and develop these skills to improve them. You are worshiping God when you put pen to paper in any effort to express your love for him or his word regardless of your skill level. Don't let your perceived lack of skill keep you from exploring and having fun. I never do, and along the way I have stumbled into some wonderful time spent connecting my whole creative being to God.

The following pages will offer a little bit of commentary and a lot of room for you to get creative as you study the Bible. I pray that you will learn to worship God through your creative gifts, whatever they may be, and I pray that God uses this study to show you new things about his character and deep love for you.

— *Anne*

# Table of Contents

Bible Study and Journaling Tips  6
Know Before You Go  8
Colossians 1 Introduction  10
Write Here, Write Now  12
The Secret Keepers  14
Drawing Near, Drawing Close  16
For Your Consideration  18
Let Us Pray  19
Colossians 2 Introduction  20
Write Here, Write Now  22
Knit Together  24
Drawing Near, Drawing Close  26
For Your Consideration  28
Let Us Pray  29
Colossians 3 Introduction  30
Write Here, Write Now  32
No Favorites  34
Drawing Near, Drawing Close  36
For Your Consideration  38
Let Us Pray  39
Colossians 4 Introduction  40
Write Here, Write Now  42
Live Wisely  44
Drawing Near, Drawing Close  46
For Your Consideration  48
Let Us Pray  49
Memory Verse Challenge  50

# Bible Study

~ **Pray and ask God to reveal himself to you as you read the Bible.** Ask for him to give you fresh wisdom about how to apply his word to your life. Ask him to open your heart and your mind to what he has to say to you, and ask him to inspire you as you worship him.

~ **Read a translation that is comfortable for you.** If you prefer a particular version, use that one. If you don't have a preference or don't know what to look for in a Bible translation, look at one passage online or through an app that offers multiple translations. Read it in several translations, and choose the one that is easiest for you to read and understand. I know many churches have a preferred translation, and it helps to do corporate study with a single version, but there is no such mandate in the Bible. From my time studying Hebrew in college, I know that I like the NKJV version for its similarity to the tone and style of the Hebrew (poetry sounds and looks like poetry; history is translated in the factual tone it was written, etc.), but I love reading the NLT for its plain language, which often helps me apply the passage to my life better. When a text is really difficult to understand, I'll read it in multiple translations because each of them will bring a different speech pattern, and my word-loving ears can find more to grab on to as I read.

~ **Try reading commentaries when you have time to dig deeper.** I love Matthew Henry's Commentary. Lots of study Bibles offer commentary alongside the text itself, and there are many good and free commentaries available through Bible apps and online. An important thing to note about commentaries is that they are the product of someone else's study, and they are not the word of God. No commentary is a perfect or complete interpretation of the Bible, but they can be excellent resources for deeper understanding and new insights.

~ **Take notes or doodle as you read.** Think back to all those book reports and time studying in school, and put those study habits to good use again. Write down words you need to look up, questions you have, themes you've seen before, phrases that stand out – anything that you want to think more about. I like sketching out things that are described in great detail as a way for me to focus on the passage and visualize the text. Genealogies can feel extremely boring, repetitive and unimportant when they feel like just a list of "begats," so I write out timelines and charts myself even though they are widely available in study books. The practice keeps my brain engaged with the material.

~ **Imagine that you are a detective looking for clues and connections.** As a writer I know that an author crafts their work and only includes things that are important to them or to the story, so I like to imagine myself as an investigator thinking about why specific details were included and why some were left out.

~ **Think of the Bible as a single, unified story.** How does the passage you are reading fit in with the big picture? Study the details, and then zoom out and ask yourself a few questions. What did I learn about God? What did I learn about my human place in God's big picture story? What can I apply to my life from this passage or verse? These questions are a good way to develop the mindset that all of the Bible is relevant to our daily lives.

~ **Creativity is worship.**  God created us in his image, and he is first and foremost the Creator.  You were created to create.

~ **Gather your supplies.**  You don't need fancy art supplies or bespoke journals to write and draw in – just some basics and any old notebook will do.  I have a letter sized blank notebook for drawing and a lined journal book for note writing.  I keep a set of highlighters, a plain black ink pen, and colored pencils in a zipper pouch that I can pick up and take with me anywhere.  I mostly work at my desk, but I've been known to find a quiet spot on the porch, spread out books and notebooks all over the bed, or head to favorite coffee shop and work.  I keep everything in my writing bag when I'm not using it (because I have a bag for everything – it's a sickness – and I am a mess who can't find things if I don't religiously put them in the same place), so it's easy to grab and get down to studying.  If you make it easy to find your supplies, it's easier to get started and to build a daily habit.

~ **There is no wrong way to journal or create.**  Everyone has a unique process for thinking of new ideas and putting them on paper.  I'll share prompts, but as you go, you will discover your own process.  You will start to see ideas beyond the prompts that you want to pursue, and that's a great thing!  Go "off book" without any regret when that happens.  If you come back to the book prompt, great.  If not, that's also great because you're creating.  If you never go beyond the study prompts, don't worry because you're still creating.

~ **Technique can be learned.**  Do you want to paint, but you haven't touched a paintbrush since water coloring in elementary school?  It's never too late to learn something new.  We won't be good at everything we try on our very first try, but don't forget that practicing a skill is an act of worship.  Every time we hone our skills through practice or learn new creative skills, we are practicing spiritual discipline.  Even if you are never very good at a specific technique, you will learn more about yourself and honor God through the effort.

~ **Don't let other people's work intimidate you.**  There are a million and four great ideas to use as inspiration online, but that can also make us feel like we won't measure up to all those beautiful images.  We won't.  But those images won't measure up to your work, either.  Rejoice that there are beautiful examples of God's creative gifts all over the internet, and then focus on your own creative work as the act of worship it's meant to be.  God treasures what we offer him with our whole hearts, whatever that may be.

~ **Have fun.**  Don't be afraid to simply get out crayons and make bold splashes of color and find the joy of making your mark.  Creating is most often a joyful act for me, and I believe that's what God intended for all of us.  There is such tremendous joy in expressing what God teaches me through his word.  It draws my heart closer to him in the most intimate way as he inspires my work.  At its best, it feels like a conversation, and I pray you have that experience, too.

*and Journaling Tips*

~ The book of Colossians was a letter written by Paul to the church at Colossae.

~ The letter was most likely written around 60 AD while Paul was in jail in Rome.

~ Colossae was a merchant town on a trade route with Rome. It was likely involved in wool production and weaving, though it's importance was beginning to fade by the time Paul wrote this letter.

~ Colossae was located in what is modern-day Turkey, about 100 miles east of Ephesus in the Lycus River Valley.

~The church at Colossae was mostly made up of Gentile (non-Jewish) believers, and they were struggling with heresy (a fancy word for incorrect theology).

*Colossians*

# Know Before You Go

In the first chapter of Colossians, Paul sets out to remind us just exactly who Jesus is. "Christ is the visible image of the invisible God. He existed before anything was created and is supreme over all creation." (Colossians 1:15 NLT) We learn that he is the creator of all things, and he holds everything together. Did you know that physicists are looking for the "God particle" - the force or tiny bit of matter that holds even the tiniest parts of an atom together? I imagine the deeper they get into that mystery, the more scientific questions it will open because we know who and what is holding everything in place—Jesus!

Jesus is central to and supreme over all creation, and he reconciled, or saved, all of creation through his sacrifice. There is no other way to be whole and acceptable to God except through Jesus—there is no other intermediary, no other path. Jesus is the embodiment and fullness of God. And we know the secret that Christ lives in you (Col. 1:27)! So, if Jesus creates everything, holds it all together, redeems everything, and lives in you… Jesus is inside you holding you together! It may be tough to remember some days, but never forget that!

Another wonderful thing we see in Paul's example is that we can and should encourage the good work happening in each other, regardless of who started it. The church at Colossae was planted by someone else—Epaphras—but Paul was faithful to cultivate the church and love it as his own. We, likewise, are a community without boundaries, all connected by faith in Jesus Christ, without exceptions—another example of Jesus at the center of it all.

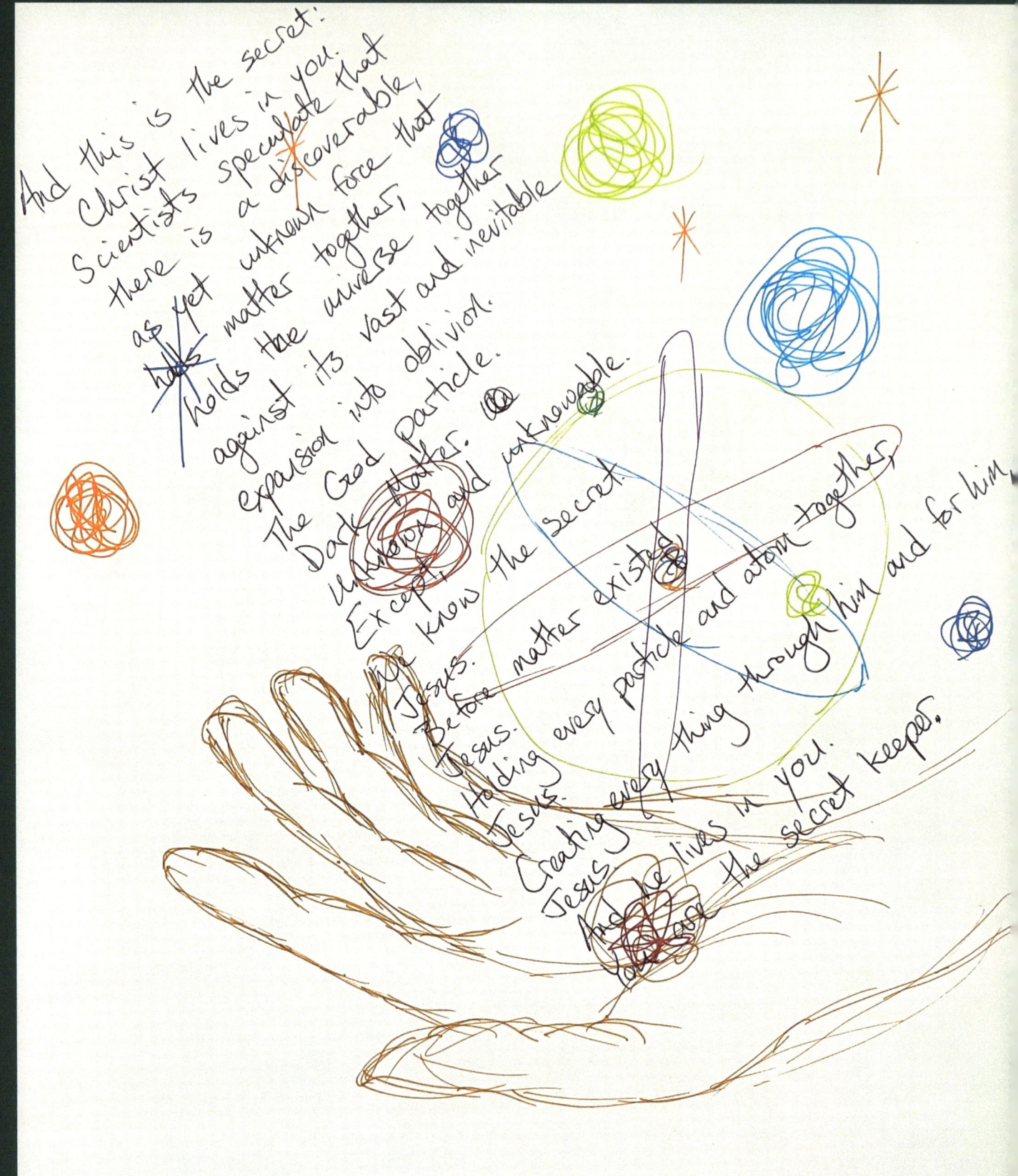

# Colossians 1

If you are new to Bible study, or even if this is old hat for you, start by praying for God to open your eyes and your heart to hear him and see him clearly in what you read. Ask him to guide you to insight about who he is and how you can apply what you're reading to your life. My pastor is fond of asking, "How will you be different because of what you read today?" God's word is alive and will always change us and mark us as his.

A few notes as we start our creative journey through Colossians: notice that in the very first verse, Paul is pointing out that he is an apostle "by the will of God." Paul, like all of us who are called by him was sent **by God** to tell others about Jesus; it had nothing to do with Paul's desires or qualifications. He also includes Timothy in his opening line to the Colossians. Timothy was like his "junior partner," so including him here is an important example.

You are not only called by God to tell the world around you about Jesus, but you are also called by God to model humility and to mentor someone less experienced in faith than you. Who are you bringing up with you, and with whom are you sharing all the amazing things God is teaching you? The whole point of being an apostle is to spread God's love. If you never pass it on, are you an effective apostle? Watch how Paul expands this idea in verses 28 and 29.

Before we leave the introduction of the letter, look closely at verse 2. Paul notes that he is writing to the believers in Colossae, *"who are faithful brothers and sisters in Christ."* What follows is a prayer for the Colossian believers to be full of God's wisdom and strength and joy. I love that Paul recognizes the community of Christ as both intimate - we are brothers and sisters - and global. The same Good News that unites us with our local church is the same Good News that unites the church all over the world, regardless of borders, denominations, or languages. We are a community without boundaries, all connected by faith in Jesus Christ.

The rest of this chapter lays out the supremacy of Christ as central to creation and salvation. I challenge you to read verses 15-22 out loud and meditate on them. There is so much to process there that I'm convinced our finite brains can only get a glimpse of the depth of this knowledge, no matter how much we study it.

# Write Here

The Kingdom of God is often represented in allegory by a planted field. In the case of Colossae, Epaphras planted seeds, and Paul helped to water them. Sometimes we struggle to do this work together, either because we are too proud to do "menial" work like watering, or because we feel inadequate to add to the work someone else did to establish the field. Look at your own ministry - are you planting seeds? You should be, even if you won't be the one to water the field or harvest the fruit. Are you watering any fields, even if you weren't the one who did the planting?

God calls us all where we are *right now* to be good gardeners: planting seeds in unbelievers, and caring for the plants growing up around us. Examine your gardening practices. Are you growing? Are you helping those around you to grow? What needs to change for you to be a better gardener? It doesn't have to be complicated. Maybe you need to start talking about your faith more. Maybe you need to build more or stronger relationships within the church to keep you connected to the body of Christ.

**Write a poem or a paragraph about your work in God's fields. Take this creative time to connect with God and listen for his direction.**

Colossians 1:24-29 tell us that God has a secret that was kept in generations past, but now is revealed. Secret societies, religious sects, cults, etcetera have mysteries that initiates are not privy to until they reach an inner circle or higher level of membership and understanding. God turned this upside down by splitting the veil that covered the mystery with Jesus's crucifixion. Under the old law, priests and sacrifices were necessary to connect to God; now through the grace of Jesus's sacrifice, we are directly connected to him. Christ lives in you! You have direct access to the mystery, the secret. There are no inner circles or higher levels beyond your relationship with Jesus and your relationship to his Body.

**Write a poem or a paragraph about the secret and the revelation of the secret. Use,** *"And this is the secret: Christ lives in you,"* **as your last line.**

*Write Now*

# The Secret

I love a good puzzle or mystery. I love ideas so big that I can't even wrap my head around them. I love when giant science ideas and giant faith ideas come together and make such a glorious swirling of theories that I can't tell where the science ends and the Bible begins. I feel all of that wonderment when I read the first chapter of Colossians.

"Christ is the visible image of the invisible God. He existed before anything was created and is supreme over all creation, for through him God created everything in the heavenly realms and on earth. He made the things we can see and the things that we can't see – such as thrones, kingdoms, rulers, and authorities in the unseen world. Everything was created through him and for him. He existed before anything else, and he holds all creation together." (Colossians 1:15-17 NLT)

Read John 1:1-5 NLT now: "In the beginning the Word already existed. The Word was with God, and the Word was God. He existed in the beginning with God. God created everything through him, and nothing was created except through him. The Word gave life to everything that was created, and his life brought life to everyone. The light shines in the darkness, and the darkness can never extinguish it."

Now go all the way back to the beginning. "In the beginning God created the heavens and the earth. The earth was formless and empty, and darkness covered the deep waters. And the Spirit of God was hovering over the surface of the waters." (Genesis 1:1-2 NLT) As you read the rest of the creation story, imagine it now even more richly with Jesus as the creator alongside God the Father.

These echoes that reverberate from the beginning to the end of the Bible are my favorite mystery in the sense that a mystery is a secret that remains hidden or unexplained. I can try for the rest of my life to understand how God and Jesus and the Spirit are three and also one. I can try for the rest of my life to understand God's secret revealed by the resurrection of Jesus is that he lives in me. But no matter how hard I try, I will barely ever scratch the surface of these big ideas.

## And this is the secret:

# Keepers

Astrophysics always fascinates me – how the universe is so big scientists think it must go on forever, how it is always in motion, and how we can only calculate estimates for the number of stars and galaxies that lie beyond our limited field of vision. If you subscribe to the Big Bang Theory as the beginning of the universe and try to leave God as creator out of it, there's still no scientific explanation for where all that compressed matter that created the universe-creating explosion came from in the first place. But we know the secret. God, through Jesus, created everything and calls each star by name – even the ones we don't even know exist yet.

The science doesn't contradict my faith; it only reinforces that I already know the secret scientists are searching for, like the God particle. Did you know that scientists were looking for a particle that explains how atoms have mass and hold together? The official name for it is the Higgs boson, but it got nicknamed "the God particle." The best part of this story to me is that the nickname wasn't intentionally religious, but it fits perfectly with the Bible's story of Christ creating everything and holding it all together.

I am always awed by those glimpses of truth, of faith and science overlapping and telling the same story. God's story is infinite, bigger than the cosmos, outside of time and space as we know it, and yet somehow still intimately concerned with the details of our lives. The God who spoke all of creation into existence wants to hear us speak to him. He loves us so deeply that he created each of us uniquely and rescued us from our sinful nature by sending Jesus to redeem us. No matter how far out into the universe we look or how deep into the particles of atoms we search, we know the secret – Jesus created all of it, and he's holding all of it together.

What does it mean for our lives to be secret keepers? It means we have a sacred duty, just like the one Paul felt in his bones, to share what we know about the truth of God - who he is, what he's done for us, how he rescued us. It means we have peace at the heart of all our knowledge. Scientific theories change all the time, politics shift in the wind, and governments crumble. Jesus will never change, will never let go of the infinite threads holding everything together, will never stop loving you. We can rest in that.

## Christ lives in you.

# Drawing Near

We are all connected by faith in Jesus Christ; we are all individuals, yet members together of the unified Body of Christ. In a single line, without lifting your pen or pencil, draw your brothers and sisters in Christ - from your church, from your neighborhood, your state, your country, the world... As you draw, pray for them. Meditate on our unbreakable bond in Christ. Notice that in this single line of pigment, all believers are connected in the singular person of Jesus and his sacrifice. Notice that in this simplicity there is no separation in us - no black or white or brown; no African, American, Asian, European; no us and them. Jesus rescued us all.

Christ is before all things, created all things, holds all things together, and reconciles all of creation through him. Jesus is the physical, visible image of the invisible Father God, and yet he is somehow distinct from the Father. As you meditate on Colossians 1:15-23, what images or words come to mind? We all think of Jesus as the man on the cross, but have you ever thought of him as the creator as well? What do you think it means that Jesus "holds all creation together?" Sketch what God shows you.

*Drawing Close*

# For Your Consideration:

Who are you bringing up with you, and with whom are you sharing all the amazing things God is teaching you?

We are all workers in God's garden fields. What job do you have right now and how effectively are you working as an apostle?

Is there a job God has called you to do before that you refused to do because you felt like it was too small a job? What does it say about our connection to the community of Christ (and so our connection to Jesus himself) when we are unwilling to serve?

Is there a job God has called you to do that felt too big, and so you avoided or refused the work? Do you think God can ever call you to something he won't equip you to handle? Or does God send us big dreams that he equips us for as we work in faith?

How often do you sit and meditate on the mysteries of God, like the secret that Jesus holds everything together or that he lives in you? How do you feel about big ideas like that?

Paul tells us that through the blood of Jesus, we can be in God's presence "holy and blameless as you stand before him without a single fault." Do you think this promise is only for heaven, or do you think that we should live with this knowledge as true now - true the moment we decided to follow Christ? Would changing your mindset about how holy and blameless you are as a forgiven believer change how you think and act in your life?

Paul says that he wants to present each person he shares the Good News with to God and for them to be perfect in their relationship to Christ. Do you think "perfect" in this context means that the believers he presents don't sin any more, or do you think it means that they are complete and mature in their faith? Are you helping anyone else to become more complete and mature in faith?

Dear Heavenly Father, may you give us your grace and peace. Show us how to live as a community of believers in our homes, in our churches, in our neighborhoods, and all across the world. Thank you for blessing us with this deep connection. Thank you for the Good News that Jesus came to rescue us and for making that same Good News spread through the world.

We ask for you to give us the spiritual wisdom and understanding that Paul prayed for so that we may honor and please you with our lives. We ask you to help us grow deeper in understanding your mysteries so that we may know you more and more. We ask you to help us stand firm in your truth without drifting away so that we may continue to share your truth.

Jesus, help us to share your secret and teach the mystery that you live in us to everyone in the world around us. Give us courage to share our faith stories boldly. Give us words when we feel afraid or inadequate to share your truth.

Give us a passion for teaching those in our sphere of influence what it means to follow you. Use our lives and our sufferings as examples to glorify you. Show us who you would have us to follow and learn from like Timothy did from Paul. Allow us to humbly walk with and learn from those who know you more deeply. Show us who we should help grow and develop in the same way that Paul taught Timothy, and help us to be good and faithful teachers of your word.

Lord, thank you for taking away our sins through the sacrifice of Jesus. Show us any sinful ways we hold in our lives so that we may confess them and turn back to your path. Thank you for the peace of your reconciliation.

Thank you for revealing your secret through Christ and for including us in your story. Let us, the secret keepers, live worthy of your calling on our lives.

God knit me together
　stitched all my tangled parts into one coherent whole
God knit us together
　you and me bound by the single thread of
　　Jesus' blood
One body knit together - buried, baptized,
　raised anew - every sinew stitched
　with the singular purpose of
　stretching ever closer to Christ.

I want them
to be encouraged
and knit together
by strong ties of love,
I want them to have
complete confidence
that they understand
God's mysterious plan,
which is Christ himself.
Colossians 2:2

# Colossians 2

While chapter 1 is all about the mystery of faith and God's secret plan being revealed in Jesus, chapter 2 continues the idea of connection. Paul deepens the theme that Jesus holds everything together and develops that idea in several ways.

The first five verses of Colossians 2 express Paul's desire for believers to be "knit together by strong ties of love" and encouraged and confident in understanding God's plan. The imagery of being knit together is such a strong visual for the relationships we need to be healthy spiritually, mentally, and emotionally. As a single thread, we're not very strong or useful, but as a network of threads knit together, we are supported by the threads around us. We can take on greater work and provide comfort and warmth to the body of Christ.

Verse 7 provides a building block plan for our connection to Christ. Our faith must be rooted in Jesus, then built on him, then established in faith as we grow in our walk, and then overflowing with thankfulness. The root imagery brings to mind a tree structure. If you are missing any one of the foundational pieces, you don't have a tree - maybe not even a shrub. It may look okay on the outside, but collapse is inevitable if you skip a step or neglect any part of the structure.

The rest of the chapter carries on the theme of connection with the image of Jesus as the head of the body. Paul describes those who have sinful minds and who are leading people off into "empty philosophies and high-sounding nonsense" as not connected to Christ. That makes sense, doesn't it? If we remain rooted in him, our thought patterns and beliefs are intimately connected with our knowledge and experience of Jesus. It can be easy to get carried away by impressive sounding arguments and persuasive words, and it's easy to find opinions that seem to make a lot of sense. Paul gives us a simple test for truth: does it come from Christ? Does it line up with what you know about Jesus and what you read in the Bible? Does it line up with the secret plan of Christ living in you? If not, it doesn't matter how smart the idea sounds or how renowned the speaker is - they're wrong.

We are free and complete in Jesus. Paul emphatically tells the Colossians not to let man-made rules or traditions get in the way of truly following Jesus; he's the only source for rules or traditions that matter. His death on the cross "disarmed the spiritual rulers" by removing the barriers between us and God. Jesus became our high priest in that moment and remains the only authority. The rules we make up seem like a good idea at the time because they are based on physical discipline, which seems so very pious of us. The problem is, those physical disciplines miss their intended target and do nothing to change our hearts. Only Jesus can do that.

# Write Here

Colossians 2:11-12 offers a beautiful juxtaposition of the Old Testament law versus the New Testament promise of salvation through Jesus. Paul uses the tradition of circumcision to show that the old laws are only effective as outward symbols of inner faith. Circumcision now that Jesus has come and died for our sins must be a "spiritual circumcision - the cutting away of your sinful nature." We also get an emphatic reminder of who does all the work of giving us new life. Check out all of the action verbs in verses 13-15: made alive, forgave, wiped out, took away, nailed, disarmed, triumphed... Whew! I'd be exhausted, except... how many of those verbs are attributed to us? Not a single one. Our faith is the result of God's work of grace through Jesus. Furthermore, we are free from man-made rules and traditions through the saving work of Jesus. Jesus is now the only source that matters for rules and traditions.

What's the silliest or craziest "rule" you believed or followed before you knew better - before you knew that Christ's law is freedom? What is a "rule" you see that doesn't really come from the Bible but is still practiced in your church? Are there any rules that you're not sure about - are they Biblical or human in origin?

**Make a list of the rules we aren't required to follow but seemed like a good idea at the time. Make another list of rules you'd like to understand and get to the bottom of so you can decide if they are worthy of following or not.**

"If you can't explain it simply, you don't understand it well enough." - Albert Einstein

Paul warns us not to be led off course by "empty philosophies and high-sounding nonsense." Think about what we have learned about Jesus so far in the book of Colossians. Now think of how you would explain it on a level that a child can understand. Avoid words that assume a working knowledge of church terminology or theology.

**Write a paragraph in simple terms to explain what you know about Jesus.**

*Write Now*

Knitting is a surprisingly recurrent theme in the Bible - Psalm 139, Job 10, and now here in Colossians 2 - and my crafter's heart loves the thought of a single thread being looped together to form strong fabric that brings warmth and comfort to our lives. Paul wants the believers in Colossae to be "knit together by strong ties of love." What a beautiful picture of the Body of Christ!

Beyond that picture of a body of believers knit together in love, there is deep meaning in Colossians 2:2-10 for those of us who are walking through suffering. I make no secret of the fact that I struggle with depression, and I have walked through horrible loss in my journey to have a child. I only survived loss and continue to survive depression because I am stitched tightly into the fabric of the Body, and I am firmly rooted in Jesus. All of my mental health tools tie back to this connection.

As humans, we crave connection – we were designed for community. Scientists who study such things have learned that in mice studies, isolation causes erratic behavior and depression symptoms. Psychologists have been urging prisons to consider solitary confinement to be a form of torture because of the ongoing havoc it wreaks on mental health. Again, science confirms what we learn from the Bible.

We need foundational truths to build our lives on in order to connect fully with other believers. With that in mind, take some time to dwell on verse 3, verse 7, and verse 10. Christ holds "all the treasures of wisdom and knowledge," he is fertile soil to let our roots grow deep and strong, and he makes us complete. As foundations go, that's as strong as it gets: unshakable, unchangeable, complete. When I'm deep in depression symptoms, solid ground is hard to come by. This passage is solid ground to build on when my emotions and thoughts are telling me lies about my worth and

*You are complete through*

# Knit Together

my work. Even depression brain can't argue with someone who holds all the treasures of wisdom and knowledge.

As followers of Christ, we all follow the same basic principles, even when we differ on the details of theology. This gives us a basis for strong ties of love within our faith community. I can guarantee you that I don't agree 100% with anyone in my family or in my church, but we can still love well and be intimately connected enough to encourage and support each other. We are deeply rooted in the truth, and those common roots tie us together to Jesus. I mentioned earlier that mice studies showed that interaction and community were positive influences on mental health. We humans are no different; strong relationship ties have a positive effect on our mental health, too.

When we are knit together as Paul describes, we form a safety net for each other. When one member of our community is struggling, the rest of us can pick up the slack and offer encouragement. We can walk alongside someone as they struggle or grieve and offer whatever support they need. We can love each other well and encourage each other to use our strengths and build our weaknesses into things that glorify God as much as or more than our strengths. Being knit together implies a close bond and deep knowledge of each other as well as deep knowledge of Jesus. Paul wants that real community for his people, and I do, too!

We are complete beings individually when we are unified **with** Christ, and we are a complete organism as the Church when we are unified **in** Christ. We need true community because it is baked into our DNA physically as humans and spiritually as members of the Body of Christ. (For more on the Body as a unified organism, read I Corinthians 12.)

*your union with Christ.*

# Drawing Near

Think about verse 3 equating Jesus to the keeper of the treasure. My brain immediately pictures treasure chests and maps. Now think about the foundation steps of verse 7 in terms of landmarks on a treasure map. Draw a treasure map that starts at accepting Jesus as your savior and ends with the hidden treasures of knowledge and wisdom. What dangers should you show on your map to avoid? What landmarks will help you point out the way to the treasure?

Draw a picture of you and Jesus "breaking the rules" together. Which "rule" that you listed in the writing prompt do you think Jesus would find most absurd? You should probably draw that one.

*Drawing Close*

# For Your Consideration:

Paul links the ideas of being "knit together by strong ties of love" with confidently understanding God's secret plan - Jesus. How do you think strong faith community relationships help us to be confident secret keepers?

Have you ever been swayed by a smooth-talker that led you away from the Bible's teachings? How long did it take you to realize they weren't speaking God's truth into your life? What did you learn about how to spot persuasive arguments or how to compare them to Biblical truth through that experience?

In verse 6, Paul reminds us that accepting Jesus as our Lord is not just a one-and-done type of action. We must continue to follow him every day. How can you make following Jesus every day a daily focal point in your life?

We are to be rooted in Christ, built on him, established in faith, and overflowing with thankfulness. Each of these steps builds up to the next like a scaffold. Do any of your foundations need attention to remain strong or to continue to grow in step with the other scaffolding pieces in your faith?

You are complete as a believer the moment you are united with Christ. Take time to reflect on what that means beyond your growth in faith. Do you struggle to feel adequate in certain areas of your life? What if you changed how you think about those perceived inadequacies and you looked at them as redeemed - united with Christ?

Paul describes spiritual circumcision as Jesus cutting away our old sinful nature, and he tells us that physical circumcision is no longer necessary now that God has revealed Jesus to be his secret plan. We get the picture here of the old law, or Old Testament, being fulfilled in Jesus, the New Testament. Where else have you noticed these parallels between the Old and New Testaments as you read the Bible?

What does it mean for you and your experience of church to know that we have complete freedom from tradition in Christ? Do you think that means that all of our traditions have no real value? Or do you think that we must continually evaluate the reason behind the tradition?

*Dear Jesus, thank you for holding all the mysteries and treasures of wisdom in your hands and for sharing them with us when we follow you. Thank you for being a foundation for our faith: nourishment for our roots, truth to build on, and the source of everything we have to be thankful for.*

*We ask for you to give us discernment to see through empty philosophies that sound good but come from human thinking rather than your truth. May we be complete in you and see those falsehoods quickly and without following them down a wrong path. Continue to cut away our sinful nature so that our new lives in you may shine as bright examples of your love and grace.*

*Holy Spirit, thank you for drawing believers together with strong ties of love. Thank you for filling us with the love of God so much that it can pour out of us and into the lives of those around us. We ask you to lead us to members of the Body of Christ who need support and strengthening and prompt us to reach out with acts of service and love. We ask you to humble our spirits and allow us to receive support and encouragement from others.*

*Heavenly Father, thank you for freeing us from man-made tradition. Thank you for fulfilling the Old Testament traditions and laws through Jesus. Give us wisdom to examine our rules and practices and hold them up to your truth and grace. Give us wisdom to pursue discipline and excellence tempered with insight to know if we have veered off into unnecessary rules.*

*Lord, thank you for giving us freedom for our souls through the death of and resurrection of Jesus. Thank you for canceling our record of sins and for nailing the charges against us to the cross.*

*Thank you for raising us to new life and perfect freedom when we trusted Christ. Let us continue to trust Christ to conquer our sinful desires and to follow the prompting of the Holy Spirit to repent and return to you.*

I stand here every day in front of this closet and consider all the things I have to wear. I examine the clothes and think about how the will fit my mood or my activity or the way my bo feels today. But really, I make a choice every day abou what I put on and what I take off and what never ever makes it to my closet for consideration in the first pla I must choose mercy and love and humility and kindness.

I must take off anger and greed and envy like dirty clothes and leave them in the heap of things tha no longer suit this new creation of Christ, bathed anew in morning merc

Since God chose you to be the holy people he loves, you must clothe yourselves with tenderhearted mercy, kindness, humility, gentleness, and patience. Above all, clothe yourselves with love, which binds us together in perfect harmony. Colossians 3:12,14

# Colossians 3

Chapter 3 is all about how to live the new life that Jesus died to give us. The first two verses give us immediate action orders: seek and set your mind on things above. These are continual actions, not just a one-time course correction when we decide to follow Jesus, and then we're done. Mindset is a discipline we must practice every day, and we are to constantly set heavenly things as the focus of our love - not earthly things. Think of this as quality (eternal, heavenly ideals) versus quantity (possessions you may acquire on earth). Maybe we can point out more physical things we want to pursue on earth, but the intangible treasures of heaven will last forever while physical treasure decays and disappears.

Next, Paul teaches us that our real lives are "hidden with Christ in God" and our true lives will be revealed through the revelation of Jesus. This feels like a giant idea to grasp. Simply stated, Jesus created each of us and holds the key to our true gifts and identity. As we grow deeper into God, more of that true identity is revealed as Christ is revealed more and more in our life's focus. When we seek God's glory first with our lives, we will share in Jesus's glory.

Colossians 3:5-14 call us to get rid of - put to death, take off - the old sin in our lives. If we strip off and burn all of our old clothes, we are left exposed and unprotected. So we need new habits - new clothes - to replace the old. We must put to death the sin in our lives. If we allow sin to continue to live as part of our lifestyle, we will stop living, certainly spiritually but many times also physically. Sin is an enemy combatant, and what we don't kill will kill us. There's a reason Paul calls the word of God a sword (Ephesians 6:10-17, Hebrews 4:12); we need a sharp weapon to put sin to death.

As we put on our new wardrobe and learn to be like Jesus, we get to toss the grubby old clothes and choose from a closet full of "tenderhearted mercy, kindness, humility, gentleness, and patience" and "above all," love. Imagine the Body of Christ as a cohesive single organism putting on such magnificent apparel! Imagine what our families and churches and neighborhoods will look like when we consistently put away sin and put on our new habits.

The last section of chapter 3 can be difficult to tackle because it takes on our roles within families and society. As we look more closely at those verses, pay special attention to the verses that set up the household instructions (Colossians 3:16-17) and the verses that conclude them (Colossians 3:23-25). Paul essentially repeats himself, which makes the idea of working for the Lord central to the household setup. If we fill up our lives with the richness of Jesus and do everything as if we are working for the Lord, every aspect of our lives, from our jobs to our homes to our hobbies, will fall into God's plan of grace.

# Write Here

Read Colossians 3:16-17 closely. Paul gives us the only standard we will ever need for our behavior - one that replaces every man-made rule with a single thought. Whatever you do, do it for God. Whatever you do - work, housekeeping, caring for your family, practicing a skill - do it as if God is your only audience to please. It can be hard to recognize this calling in the midst of tedious work or piles of dishes, but God deeply cares about every aspect of our lives and wants everything we do, no matter how small and simple it seems to us, to glorify him and tell his story.

Verse 16 is the basis for this standard: "Let the message about Christ, in all its richness, fill your lives." We should use this wisdom to teach and encourage each other and to sing thankful songs to God. Paul doesn't care about whether anyone in Colossae can carry a tune or play a single note on an instrument. Our lives are music, and our actions make it a sweet sound or a cacophony.

**Write a song (and if you feel led, sing it out loud when you're done writing) to teach us about what God is telling your heart about verses 16-17.**

Think about Colossians 3:18-4:1 as an operational flow chart. If you need to, sketch out what your current organizations look like - family, work, church, etc.

**Write an analysis of those operations. What are their organizational strengths? What are their weaknesses? How can you work within the organization's structure to make it stronger, more efficient, more representative of Christ? Honestly write out your questions and/or frustrations with the archetype we have to work with. Pray for God to lead you to Biblical answers, and seek out wise Christians you can discuss with.**

*Write Now*

# No Favorites

Colossians 3:18-4:1 tend to be a thorny, uncomfortable lot to talk about, so let's take some time to really understand them well. Verse 18 is one that is often very offensive to women, and I understand why. It has been taken out of context, abused, and misrepresented. You may still find it offensive after this discussion, but it's still the word of God. I ask you to meditate on the actual words, and pray for God's wisdom to help you understand them and apply them in your life.

Submit here means submit. There's no way around that. But it's more along the lines of willingly submitting to a government authority. It's actually a military term referring to voluntarily organizing under a commanding officer. I find that illustration to be the most helpful in understanding the idea of submission. When two equal commanding officers come together to fight a battle, they can comfortably share command... to a point. One of them will have to have the final say on the battlefield should any difference in orders between the two arise, or their troops will be in total disarray. This voluntary submission is a choice - an action that doesn't infer inferiority or blind obedience.

We have been given the archetype of Adam and Eve, with Adam created first and given the job of naming all the animals and tending to the Garden of Eden, and Eve created next to be his helpmate (a partner comparable to him). Someone has to be the head of the organization, and in the case of families, every example in the Bible says that head is to be the husband. When an organization works well, it looks like a machine in which all the parts are of equal importance. Each are necessary, and none are inferior in quality or in workmanship.

This command structure in no way applies to single women or outside the home. You are the solitary commander of your troops unless you decide to join forces with another commander at some point. As a single woman, you are called to submit to any legitimate and applicable governing authorities. We are **ALL** called to **submit to one another in love** (Ephesians 5:21). Women are now and always have been called to perform vital spiritual and civic leadership roles - look at the examples of Deborah, Esther, Rahab, and Ruth, to name a few. Paul also praised and thanked women who worked for Jesus; several of those were well known business owners. So the Bible includes examples of women who particpated equally in the work of the Body.

# Christ is all that matters,

Verse 19 calls men to love their wives, with a special instruction not to treat them harshly. "Love" here implies that a husband will protect and take responsibility for his wife as well as seek out her good. As a wife, I'll accept that as an equal trade for my submission, especially in combination with the command given to husbands not treat their wives harshly. In other words, men aren't supposed to be tyrants with the power given to them by their wives' willful act of submission.

Verses 20-21 address the relationships of children and parents. As children under the care of our parent's household, we are called to obey them. As we transition to adulthood and take on our own households, we should still respect and honor our parents. Parents, specifically fathers, are called to parent gently and respectfully by not making ridiculous rules or discouraging their children. Have you ever wondered why men and women are given differently worded instructions that basically amount to the same thing? Women most often nurture; men often need help learning how to do that. Men are not excused from nurturing just because it's harder for them. In fact, the emphasis on men to love, to not be harsh, and to not aggravate their children shows us that men are to do more than just issue executive commands.

The rest of this section has been used out of context to justify horrific, ungodly institutions like slavery, apartheid, and segregation. Colossians 3:11 makes it clear that we are ALL EQUAL in Christ. Even though it has existed throughout history and is referenced in the Bible, there is no Biblical justification for slavery, racism, and discrimination. None. Paul addresses institutions in their actual form and offers practical guidance. I have no idea why God didn't tell him to denounce slavery as an evil to be eradicated. I do know that the original laws God codified for the Israelites provided for a year of Jubilee that canceled all debts and freed slaves; that system had a grace clause and a finite term built in.

What we can look at here to apply to our lives today are the actual instructions, as if the slave or bond-servant is an employee, and the master is an employer. This is excellent, practical workplace advice. Work as though you are working for the Lord. Jesus is truly our only Master. He has no favorites, so the standards apply equally to each of us, and masters here on earth will be called to give an account of their leadership to none other than Jesus.

*and he lives in all of us.*

## Drawing Near

Every makeover show features a "Before and After" segment. Think about the old and new nature that Paul describes in terms of your wardrobe. What do your old, ugly things look like as they get discarded? What do your new, beautiful clothes hanging in your new and improved closet represent? Draw what God shows you as you meditate on these images.

Draw some bullseye targets that you might use for archery or sharpshooting. Inside those targets, draw things that you know are sinful and need to be put to death in your life. Spend some time confessing those sins to God, and ask him to show you how to change your habits and put away your old sinful nature.

*Drawing Close*

# For Your Consideration:

What is your life's focus? Do you find that you are most often thinking about earthly things or heavenly things?

If our life is to be hidden with Christ in God, but we are most often acting on earthly motivations, where is our heart actually hidden? How can we improve our focus and motivation to be hidden in Christ?

God is the only audience that matters when we work, which elevates everything we do to an act of worship when we work for him. Does that change your attitude about your job or your housework or parenting?

As we put on our new nature in Jesus, we are called to learn more about him, to do our life's work for him, and to become like him. Learn. Do. Become. If you examine your life, how are you progressing? Are you consistently becoming more like Jesus? If not, what do you think you need to change?

I love new clothes. It's fun to try them on and see how great they look in the mirror. God gives us a new wardrobe full of tenderhearted mercy, kindness, humility, gentleness, patience, love, peace, thankfulness, forgiveness. Try those on and see how they look on you. Where should you wear this new outfit?

Do you struggle with the structure of authority God gives us? Does submitting your life willingly to Christ change the way you think about willingly submitting to legitimate sources of authority in your life?

We are called to be representatives of Jesus in whatever we do or say. We are called to work willingly at everything we do as if we are working for Jesus and not for people. "Whatever" encompasses every single word and action. How often do you live up to this standard? How can you be more mindful and intentional about applying this standard to every single word and action every day?

We can never live up to God's standard of perfection, which is why Jesus came to rescue us from our sin. That grace covers us. How can you add grace to your wardrobe and to your mindfulness every day?

Dear Lord Jesus, thank you for being my life - for hiding my true life in you and for sharing your glory with me. Thank you for giving us purpose in every moment and focus for every thought and motivation.

Please continue to make our old sinful nature apparent when it pops up in our lives and our actions. Help us to be quick to confess and return to you. Illuminate the behaviors and attitudes that we need to submit to your authority so that we may grow to be more like you.

Dear Heavenly Father, thank you for creating each of us as equally valuable works of art. Help us to always see Christ in each other and respect your image bearers. Let us be quick to forgive as you forgave us, and let us be gracious in our actions towards one another.

Let us always meditate on the new clothes you provided for our new natures. Holy Spirit, be ever reminding us to wear love and mercy and kindness and humility and gentleness and patience and peace and thankfulness. Unite us as one Body ruled by the love and mercy of Christ. Fill us richly with the message of Jesus so that it pours out into everything we do.

God, give us wisdom and fill us with grace to work within the family and organizational structures you provide for our good. Let us submit to one another in love and recognize that in doing so we are submitting to you. Where we are leaders, keep our pride in check and help us to be just and fair in all things.

Thank you for giving us the standard of working at all things as if we are working for you. Let us continue to find freedom in the knowledge that we are glorifying you and not trying to please people with our work.

A mind alert to the voice of God moving spiritual beings through a physical realm... to every stirring of his breath

A life devoted to the One

A heart radiating gratitude with every breath exuding Praise for the giver of all good

Devote yourselves to prayer with an alert mind and a thankful heart. Colossians 4:2

# Colossians 4

Paul ends his letter to the Colossian church with an admonition to continue earnestly in prayer. The New Living Translation says, "Devote yourselves to prayer with an alert mind and a thankful heart." (Colossians 4:2 NLT). Devotion implies a serious commitment of time and effort and passion. Paul emphasizes that we should be devoted with an alert mind and a thankful heart. That's a tall order, but a noble one. Our challenge in prayer is to quiet our minds and focus on seeking God's face. Coming to God with an attitude of thanksgiving pulls our focus back from ourselves and places it appropriately on the greatness of God and how well he has provided for us.

Paul also asks his friends to pray for him. He asks for more opportunities to speak to people about Jesus, and he asks that he would be able to share the message clearly. We don't always feel comfortable sharing our faith, but keep praying for opportunities and God will open the door for you to share what you are learning in your Bible study or what your church is doing. It may feel like small talk at first, but practicing makes it easier to open a conversation and plant a seed with someone. As you pray for more ways to share, pray also for your message to be clear and for God to give you the words you need in every situation to share his love. I promise you, if this is your prayer, God will never provide you a place to share his story without also providing the words you need. In Isaiah 55:11, God promises that he never sends his word out without it accomplishing his purpose.

Verses 5 and 6 are advice along the same lines to "live wisely" with unbelievers so that we will be able to make the most of every chance we get to share with them. "Live wisely" covers a lot of ground, but telling us to let our "conversation be gracious and attractive" sets the expectation that we should be known for our love and willing and able to share that with the world around us all the time. Christians in 60 AD were considered to be a suspicious and untrustworthy group with crazy beliefs that threatened the world's status quo... So not much has changed. We still need to let our wise talk dispel the rumors and the bad impressions the world has of Christ followers so that you will have the credibility to share your story.

I always love how Paul's letters end. He takes time to verbalize specific encouragement and to compliment the people he worked with in Colossae and beyond. He clearly loves these people and wants them to know how dear they are to him. That's a great example for us to follow in our leadership roles.

# Write Here

A thankful heart is an attitude we can develop even if it doesn't come naturally to us. If you have trouble naming specific things you are grateful to God for, then widen your focus and think bigger. Do you have a place to live? Do you have food to eat? As you list things you are grateful for, begin to draw the focus closer to your heart. How has God provided for your spiritual needs? Your emotional needs?

**Write a list of 10 things you're thankful for. Bonus writing assignment: get a notebook a begin a gratitude journal by writing down 3 things every day you can thank God for.**

Paul gives specific encouragement and praise to friends and fellow ministers. He obviously has a network of missionaries he works with as well as friends at churches he visited. What do your networks look like? How do you encourage the people within them? Imagine what our offices and homes and churches would look like if we made sharing Christ and giving specific encouragement a daily habit.

**Write out a prayer asking God to show you with whom and how you can share the mystery of Christ around you and how you can encourage the people around you on a regular basis. Bonus writing assignment: write a note of encouragement to someone you love and send it to them.**

*Write Now*

# Live

Throughout Colossians, we have learned that a life lived with Jesus at the center of it is the only kind of life we are meant to have as Christians. Paul's final advice in chapter 4 sums it all up in a single, simple phrase: Live wisely.

We know the secret plan of God that we are reconciled to him through Jesus. He created us and holds us and all of creation together. More than that, Jesus rescued us from darkness and sin and gave us freedom and life in the light through his sacrifice. Paul repeats over and over in Colossians that Christ lives in us, and that means we will share in his glory. That's the secret that's no longer hidden from the world. That's the mystery that we get to proclaim through living wisely.

Jesus holds the all the hidden treasures of wisdom and knowledge, and the key to living wisely is to grow deep roots into our study of the Bible and our relationship with Jesus. As we grow in our knowledge of the Word and of Christ, our faith grows strong. Wise faith enables us to discern the "empty philosophies" of earthly logic and speak the truth of God's love into the world.

Paul reminds us that we must consistently keep our minds focused on the things of heaven and not the things of earth. If we build habits like daily prayer and Bible study, it's a lot easier to keep heavenly things central in our thoughts. We also have to act wisely and change our old sinful habits into actions that reflect the new nature we received when we were rescued. Use that wonderful image of a closet full of the new clothes that fit your new nature: mercy, kindness, humility, gentleness, patience, love, peace, thankfulness, and forgiveness - with love above all. In fashion cliche terms, "Love is the new black." Love covers well and goes with everything, so it's always a good choice.

# Make the most of

# Wisely

If we stick to those foundations, living wisely will be a natural outpouring of God's word dwelling richly within us. As we grow in our confidence of our knowledge of God's mysterious plan, we'll have more confidence to share that message wherever we go.

We'll also find more freedom, which used unwisely can cause us to be stumbling blocks to nonbelievers. We know that the death and resurrection of Jesus stripped away the old traditions, fulfilled the old law, and brought us into complete freedom in Jesus. Living wisely in freedom means we must evaluate the "rules" and traditions of our faith in order to know if they are God-given and to be followed, if they are man-made but meaningful and Biblical, or if they are man-made in an effort to use self-denial and extreme discipline to try to make us more godly. That last category is useless because it doesn't address the root problem of sin, only the physical aspect of it. But God-given wisdom allows us to navigate freedom in a way that always honors him.

Living wisely also means we'll need to examine the organizational structures God has put us in so we can determine our role within each one. Paul gave us an outline for families, and we all have places (like work) where we have to willingly submit to a proper authority. We know that submission isn't inferiority, but a decision to follow God's plan and work hard at everything we do as if we are working for the Lord.

The more we honestly live out our faith in the world, the more evident the love of Christ will be in our lives, and the more opportunities we will have to share God's truth. Jesus said the world would know his disciples by their love for one another (John 15:35), which makes love the best part of our new wardrobe and the wisest way to live.

*every opportunity.*

# Drawing Near

How do you stay focused while you pray? I discovered a wonderful technique in the book *Praying in Color* by Sybil MacBeth. She outlines a method for doodling while you pray to keep your mind alert and focused on the things you need to pray about. Try a prayer doodle. Write the subject of your prayer in a single word in the center of the page. As you pray, draw shapes or patterns around the word as you pray.

Continue the prayer doodling by praying specifically for one person you know you should reach out to and share God's story with. Pray for opportunities to start conversations about faith. Pray for God to give you the clear message he has for that person. Pray for their heart to be ready and willing to accept God's message.

*Drawing Close*

# For Your Consideration:

How can you devote yourself to prayer? Do you need to establish a daily habit, or do you need to develop your prayer focus to seek God's face before you seek his provision?

An alert mind during prayer or meditation can be especially difficult for women. We have a fairly constant inner dialogue, and we often juggle multiple roles that vie for our attention throughout the day. Besides prayer doodling, what are some ways you can practice bringing your mind back to intentional prayer when it goes wandering?

Do you make a daily practice of gratitude? Even a simple review at the end of the day shifts our perspective to the bigger picture of what God is doing in our lives. How can you develop thanksgiving into your life at least once a day?

Paul boldly asks for more opportunities to share God's message, even after it landed him in jail. Do you pursue conversation openings that allow you to share your faith? Do you ever pray for more opportunities? If not, why do you think you don't?

God will always be faithful to use his word to accomplish his purpose, but Paul still asks the Colossians to pray for him to speak God's message clearly. Do you think we should pray for this, too? Do you think regular Bible study could also help us be more clear in our messaging?

How often do you encourage the people around you? What do you think it could do to your relationships within your family, at work, and in your church if you set out to intentionally encourage and praise people in your life? What do you think it could do for their spiritual health and mental health?

What is the biggest thing you have learned from studying Paul's letter to the church at Colossae? How will you apply that lesson in your life?

*Dear Heavenly Father, we come to you with thankful hearts and bring you the offering of our gratitude. You have provided for every single detail of our lives and given us the greatest treasure in the universe - Jesus. We praise you for revealing your secret plan.*

*God, we claim your promise that your word always produces fruit when it goes out into the world. Thank you for your faithfulness. Give us more opportunities to share your truth and love in the world around us. As we share, help us to be clear and effective messengers. Let us recall your word from our study and let us speak your truth with love that is evident and overflowing.*

*Dear Lord Jesus, you set the ultimate example of how to live wisely among unbelievers. Guide us as we strive to grow in you and become more like you. Thank you for rescuing us from the darkness of our sins. May your light shine through us as reflections of your grace.*

*Holy Spirit, come and fill us with the grace of God so that our hearts will overflow into words of grace and gratitude. Speak through us when we don't know what to say to an unbeliever, just as you intercede and pray on our behalf when we don't know what words to pray. Lead us into fruitful conversations and move in the hearts of the world around us so that they will come to know Jesus as we do.*

*Thank you, God, for continuing to speak through faithful servants like Paul. Thank you for revealing wisdom and truth when we study your word. Let us continue to dive into the spiritual disciplines of study and prayer so that we may draw ever closer to you.*

# Colossians Memory

Whatever method you use to do it, I challenge you to memorize Bible verses so that you will have a memory bank full of God's word that will make it easy for you to recall when you find yourself in need of words directly from God. Some people like to write verses longhand in journals or make them look artful with hand lettering art. Maybe you learn best with constant visual reminders like note cards you can put on your refrigerator door or your mirror. Find a way that works for you, and go for it!

*Then the way that you live will always honor and please the Lord, and your lives will produce every kind of good fruit. All the while, you will grow as you learn to know God better and better. - Colossians 1:10 NLT*

**Christ is the visible image of the invisible God. He existed before anything was created and is supreme over all creation. - Colossians 1:15 NLT**

Yet now he has reconciled you to himself through the death of Christ in his physical body. As a result, he has brought you into his presence, and you are holy and blameless as you stand before him without a single fault. - Colossians 1:22 NLT

*Let your roots grow down into him, and let your lives be built on him. Then your faith will grow strong in the truth you were taught, and you will overflow with thankfulness. - Colossians 2:7 NLT*

**So you are also complete through your union with Christ, who is the head over every ruler and authority. - Colossians 2:10 NLT**

# Verse Challenge

You have died with Christ, and he has set you free from the spiritual powers of this world. So why do you keep on following the rules of the world, such as, "Don't handle! Don't taste! Don't touch!"? Such rules are mere human teachings about things that deteriorate as we use them. These rules may seem wise because they require strong devotion, pious self-denial, and severe bodily discipline. But they prove no help in conquering a person's evil desires.  - Colossians 2:20-23 NLT

*For you died to this life, and your real life is hidden with Christ in God. - Colossians 3:3 NLT*

**In this new life, it doesn't matter if you are a Jew or a Gentile, circumcised or uncircumcised, barbaric, uncivilized, salve, or free. Christ is all that matters, and he lives in all of us.  - Colossians 3:11 NLT**

And let the peace that comes from Christ rule in your hearts. For as members of one body you are called to live in peace. And always be thankful.  - Colossians 3:15 NLT

*Work willingly and whatever you do, as though you were working for the Lord rather than for people.  - Colossians 3:23 NLT*

**Devote yourselves to prayer with an alert mind and a thankful heart. Pray for us, too, that God will give us many opportunities to speak about his mysterious plan concerning Christ. That is why I am here in chains. Pray that I will proclaim this message as clearly as I should. Live wisely among those who are not believers, and make the most of every opportunity. Let you conversation be gracious and attractive so that you will have the right response for everyone.  - Colossians 4:2-6 NLT**

For more resources from Mabbat Press,

visit

## Mabbat.Blog

for new weekly posts, to join the mailing list, and to find other books and free e-books from Mabbat Press

connect

## @mabbatblog
## @anne_weil

contact

## mabbatblog@gmail.com

for more information or to book a speaking event

www.ingramcontent.com/pod-product-compliance
Lightning Source LLC
LaVergne TN
LVHW071032070426
835507LV00003B/126